THE BRITISH MUSEUM
BOOK OF
THE
ROSETTA
STONE

THE BRITISH MUSEUM BOOK OF
THE ROSETTA STONE

Carol Andrews

Department of Egyptian Antiquities, The British Museum

Peter Bedrick Books
New York

PJ
1531
R5
A53
1985

First American edition published in 1985 by
Peter Bedrick Books, New York. Published
by agreement with British Museum Publications, Ltd.

© 1981 The Trustees of the British Museum

Library of Congress Cataloging in Publication Data

Andrews, Carol.
  The Rosetta Stone.

  1. Rosetta Stone inscription. I. Title.
PJ1531.R5A53   1985   493'.1   85-9010
ISBN 0-87226-033-X
ISBN 0-87226-034-8 (pbk.)

Printed in the United States of America

Acknowledgments

The photographs on pages 14, 37, 42, and 44 are reproduced
with the kind permission of Anna Benson Gyles.

CONTENTS

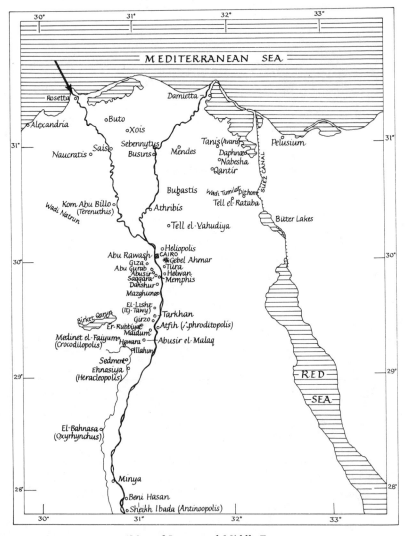

*Map of Lower and Middle Egypt
showing the city of Rosetta.*

Hieroglyphs before decipherment

On 24 August AD 394 on the island of Philae at
the southern border of Egypt hieroglyphs were
used apparently for the last time to inscribe the
ancient Egyptian language. The final inscription
on stone in demotic, the latest and most cursive
of the three scripts employed by the ancient
Egyptians, is dated less than sixty years later, to
AD 452. Although it is possible that demotic written with ink and brush or pen on papyrus was in
use a little longer, for all useful purposes during
the next 1,370 years ancient Egypt was silent, for
the art of reading her ancient scripts had been
lost. There was no one to give voice to the count-
less hieroglyphic inscriptions which swarmed all
over her monuments or to the texts in cursive
hieratic and demotic crowded on papyri and
flakes of stone and pottery. The language itself,
however, survived written in Greek letters sup-
plemented by seven signs borrowed from demotic, in a form called Coptic which is the script
and language of the Christian descendants of the
ancient Egyptians. Indeed, the word Coptic is

merely a form of Aiguptios, that is, Egyptian. Coptic as a spoken language died out in the six-teenth century AD, but it is still read in Coptic churches at the present day. Its vocabulary con-sists of a mixture of ancient Egyptian and Greek words. Of even greater importance later, early Coptic primers were written in Arabic so anyone who could read Arabic had access to the last form of the ancient Egyptian language.

Even while ancient Egyptian was a living lan-guage the Greeks and Romans made no real at-tempt to understand the scripts in which it could be written. Of ancient authorities only Clement of Alexandria writing during the second to third centuries AD made quite clear the distinction be-tween hieroglyphs, the script of official and reli-gious texts, and demotic, the script of everyday communication. In particular, the enigmatic, es-oteric and symbolic nature of hieroglyphs was stressed; cursive demotic held no interest to compare with the pictorial script in the eyes of classical writers. As early as the first century BC the Greek historian Diodorus Siculus, comment-ing on hieroglyphs, wrote: 'Now it happens that the forms of their [the Egyptians'] letters take the

shape of all kinds of living creatures and of the
extremities of the human body and of imple-
ments. . . . For their writing does not express the
intended idea by a combination of syllables, one
with another, but by the outward appearance of
what has been copied and by the metaphorical
meaning impressed upon the memory by prac-
tice. . . . So the hawk symbolises for them every-
thing which happens quickly because this
creature is just about the fastest of winged animals. And the idea is transferred, through the
appropriate metaphorical transfer, to all swift
things and to those things to which speed is appropriate.'

During the early centuries AD the adoption of
hieroglyphs by the Neo-Platonist philosophers as
a divinely inspired script symbolically embodying
all human wisdom gave rise to a body of her-
metic writings and to such tracts as Horapollo's
Hieroglyphica. That these were among the first
works on the subject to be rediscovered during
the European Renaissance is the reason for the
tradition among scholars of the sixteenth and
seventeenth centuries that hieroglyphs were
purely symbolic and contained in their signs the

The Rosetta Stone.

lost lore of ancient Egypt. The influence exer-
cised by this belief on attempts at decipherment
is best exemplified by the claims of the German
priest Athanasius Kircher who professed in a
mid-seventeenth-century work to be able to read
whole sentences in what would eventually prove
to be a single alphabetically written hieroglyphic
word.

French activities in Egypt at the end of the
eighteenth century made accessible to scholars
wrestling with the problem of the decipherment
of hieroglyphs great quantities of inscribed and
written material. Even more important, a new
school of thought was arising which rejected the
symbolic and esoteric value of hieroglyphs, real-
ising rather that they were characters used to
write an ancient language and that hieratic and
demotic were but cursive forms of the same
script. It is, consequently, almost certain that the
key to the decipherment of hieroglyphs would
have been found eventually even without the
discovery of such bilingual texts as that on the
Rosetta Stone, but it is difficult to say for how
much longer an understanding of ancient Egypt's
scripts would have been delayed.

The discovery of the Rosetta Stone

The slab of compact black basalt, called for nearly two centuries the Rosetta Stone, stands in the Egyptian Sculpture Gallery of the British Museum in London. It is named from its findplace in the Western Delta, a small village called Rashid, better known to Europeans as Rosetta, which lies a few kilometres from the sea on the Bolbinitic branch of the Nile. The circumstances of its discovery in mid-July 1799 are in some doubt. According to one version, it was just lying on the ground, but the likelier account records that it was built into a very old wall which a company of French soldiers had been ordered to demolish in order to clear the way for the foundations of an extension to the fort later known as Fort Julien. Napoleon's Map of Egypt shows Fort Julien to have stood on the west or left bank of the Nile.

The officer in charge of the demolition squad, a Lieutenant of Engineers called Pierre Francois Xavier Bouchard, and his officer companions are credited with having realised almost at once the importance of the Stone's three distinct inscriptions, namely that they were each versions of a single text in three different scripts. Since the last of the inscriptions was in Greek and could therefore be read, it was clear that it might be possible to use its translation as the key to the decipherment of the hieroglyphs in the first section. General Menou arranged to have part of the Greek section translated almost at once in order to ascertain the nature of the text.

News of the Stone's discovery and its possible importance was not made public until September 1799 in the *Courrier d'Égypte* by which time it had already been dispatched to Cairo and placed in the Institut National which Napoleon had recently founded there. On its arrival in Cairo in mid-August the Stone at once became an object of the deepest interest to the body of learned men whom Napoleon had taken with him to Egypt. The inscription between the hieroglyphic and Greek sections was soon identified by Jean-Joseph Marcel and Remi Raige as the cursive script derived from Hieroglyphs called demotic, or as they termed it, enchorial, but no progress was made in its decipherment or in that of the hieroglyphic section. It was subsequently ordered that a number of copies of the Stone's in-

An ancient block inscribed with hieroglyphs incorporated into a wall at Rosetta.

scriptions be made for distribution among the scholars of Europe, and the Institut's two skilled lithographers, Marcel and A. Galland, were instructed to make them. The method used was to cover the surface of the Stone with printer's ink, lay upon it a sheet of paper and roll india-rubber rollers over it until a good impression had been obtained. Several of these ink impressions were sent to scholars of great repute in many parts of Europe, and in the autumn of 1800 two copies were presented to citizen Du Theil of the Institut National of Paris by General Dugua on his return from Egypt.

How the Stone came to England

When Cairo was threatened after the successful operations of Sir Ralph Abercromby in Egypt in the spring of 1801, the scholars of the French expedition decided to leave the capital for the safety of Alexandria, taking with them their notes, specimens and collected antiquities, among them the Rosetta Stone. It is ironic that had they remained in the capital they would have benefited from the terms of its capitulation which would have allowed them to return to France with all the objects in their possession. Instead, by Article XVI of the Capitulation of Alexandria they were compelled to surrender the Rosetta Stone and several other large and important Egyptian antiquities to General Hutchinson at the end of August of that year. Some of these he dispatched at once to England on HMS *Admiral,* others in HMS *Madras,* but the Rosetta Stone did not leave Egypt until later in the year.

In Alexandria it had been transferred to a warehouse where it was deposited among General Menou's baggage, covered with a cloth and under a double matting. In September 1801 when

Colonel (later Major-General) Turner claimed the Stone under the terms of the treaty of capitulation the French General refused to give it up, affirming that it was his private property. Its surrender was consequently attended by some difficulty. An eye-witness account by Edward Clarke, an English traveller and antiquary, records that the Stone was handed over 'in the streets of Alexandria' by a French officer and a member of the Institut, in the presence of William Hamilton (a fellow English traveller and antiquary), a Mr. Cripps and the writer. In spite of the British military escort, the French officer advised that the Stone be removed from the city before the French troops realised what had happened.

As soon as he was in possession of the Stone Colonel Turner embarked with it on HMS *L'Égyptienne* and arrived in Portsmouth in February 1802. On 11 March the Stone was deposited at the headquarters of the Society of Antiquaries in London where it remained for a few months while the inscriptions on it were submitted to a very careful examination by a number of Oriental and Greek scholars. In July the President of the Society had four plaster casts made for the Universities of

French troops of Napoleon's Expeditionary Force parading at Rosetta.

Oxford, Cambridge, Edinburgh and Trinity College, Dublin, and had good copies of the Greek text engraved and sent to all the great Universities, Libraries, Academies and Societies of Europe. Towards the end of the year the Stone was removed from the Society of Antiquaries to the British Museum where it was mounted and immediately exhibited to the general public. It has remained on exhibition ever since.

Description of the Stone

Even in its incomplete state the Rosetta Stone is
a substantial monument, measuring 3 ft 9 in
(114 cm) in height, 2 ft 4½ in (72 cm) in width and
11 in (28 cm) in thickness. Its weight has been cal-
culated as just under ¾ of a ton (762 kg). A large
part of the left upper corner, a narrower section
of the right upper edge and the lower right
corner are missing. The top of the stone was
almost certainly rounded and would, to judge
from other Ptolemaic stelae of a similar type,
have had sculpted in its rounded section the
winged disc of Horus of Edfu with pendent
uraei, one wearing the crown of Upper Egypt,
the other the crown of Lower Egypt and each
carrying a *shen*-ring and ceremonial fan. Below
this winged disc would probably have been a
figure of the king standing in the presence of
various gods and goddesses; such a scene is at
the top of the Damanhur stela which contains a
copy of the hieroglyphic section of the Rosetta
Stone (see below). When the stone was complete
it must have been between 5 and 6 ft (152.5–
183 cm) high, and when set up near the statue of

the king in whose honour it had been carved it would have formed a prominent monument in the temple in which it was displayed.

The inscriptions on the Rosetta Stone are written in two languages, Egyptian and Greek, but in three scripts. The first of the Egyptian texts is written in HIEROGLYPHS, the formal pictorial script in use since the beginning of the First Dynasty nearly 3,000 years earlier. Hieroglyphs are used principally as a monumental script for incising into hard materials or for painting in elaborate, colourful detail on plaster or wood. They appear in almost every medium; but on papyrus from an early date they were generally superseded by HIERATIC, a cursive script derived from hieroglyphs. The second Egyptian text on the Rosetta Stone is in DEMOTIC, an extremely cursive script which evolved from abbreviated and modified hieratic and which replaced hieratic as the script for all but religious texts from about 643 BC. The Greek inscription is written in Greek capitals.

Only parts of the last 14 lines of the hieroglyphic text remain and these correspond to the last 28 lines of the Greek text which are themselves damaged. The demotic section consists of 32 lines, the first 14 being damaged at the beginnings (the text reads from right to left), and the Greek text of 54 lines of which the last 26 are damaged at the ends. Most of the missing lines in the hieroglyphic section can be restored from a copy of the decree on a stela discovered in 1898 at Damanhur, the ancient Hermopolis Parva, in the Delta and now in the Cairo Museum (no. 22188). As this copy was made fourteen years after that on the Rosetta Stone, certain clauses, which were relevant in Year 9 of Ptolemy v's reign but no longer of importance in Year 23, are omitted and can only be reconstructed from the demotic section. A further version of the Rosetta Stone's text, dated to Year 21 of Ptolemy v, was incised on the walls of the Birth House of the temple of Isis on the island of Philae.

The earlier decipherers of the Rosetta Stone

The earliest translation in English of the Greek text on the Rosetta Stone was read by the Reverend Stephen Weston before the Society of Antiquaries in London in April 1802. A French translation had already been made by citizen Du Theil using the ink impressions presented to the Institut National by General Dugua. Du Theil revealed that the Stone was 'a monument of the gratitude of some priests of Alexandria, or some neighbouring place, towards Ptolemy Epiphanes'; a Latin translation by citizen Ameilhon appeared in Paris shortly afterwards in January 1801.

The first studies of the demotic text were those of a French orientalist, A. I. Silvestre de Sacy, and a Swedish diplomat, J. D. Åkerblad. In 1802 Silvestre de Sacy succeeded in identifying in the demotic version the equivalents of some of the proper names which occurred in the Greek section, namely Ptolemy, Arsinoe, Alexander and Alexandria. Åkerblad carried these results a little further by identifying all the remaining

Thomas Young FRS (1773–1829).

proper names in the demotic text and by recog-
nising the alphabetically written words for 'temples' and 'Greeks' and the pronominal suffix for
'him' and 'his'. Unfortunately, both Silvestre de
Sacy and Åkerblad laboured under the great
misapprehension that because the demotic words
which they had deciphered were alphabetically
written all demotic words were exclusively alphabetic.

The credit for being the first to recognise that
Egyptian writing consisted of both alphabetic and
non-alphabetic signs belongs to the Englishman
Thomas Young (1773–1829), author of the
'Undulatory Theory of Light'. Young was a phy-
sician and physicist with an amazing knowledge
of languages who first became interested in
Egyptology and the Egyptian language after
reading an article which mentioned the Rosetta
Stone and its unknown language. His earliest
work, however, was on a damaged funerary papyrus written in cursive or linear hieroglyphs. It
was not until the summer of 1814 that he took a copy
of the Rosetta Stone's demotic section with him
on his annual visit to Worthing on the south
coast. Young soon realised the fallacy of Åkerblad's alphabetic theory for demotic and, even

more importantly, he grasped the fact that hieroglyphs and demotic were closely related. His earlier studies of hieratic and linear hieroglyphic documents soon led him to realise that hieratic too was a script derived from hieroglyphs.

With the Rosetta Stone his method was to find a word in the Greek text which occurred more than once and then to look for a group of signs in the demotic section which occurred approximately an equal number of times. The group which occurred in nearly every line he decided must be demotic for 'and'. After this the groups which appeared most frequently were equated with the words 'king', 'Ptolemy' and 'Egypt'. Then he wrote the Greek equivalents over the groups of demotic signs identified. Thus Young obtained some probable demotic identifications with translatable Greek words written in regularly throughout the demotic version. Filling in the gaps must have been extremely difficult. He was further hindered by the inscription being incomplete and the fact that the demotic text was not a literal translation of the Greek nor the Greek a literal translation of the demotic. Nevertheless, it was not long before Young's Greek-demotic vocabulary amounted to eighty-six groups of signs, mostly correct in identification though nearly all incorrect in transliteration.

He then proceeded to demonstrate the fact, guessed long before by C.J. de Guignes and J. Zoëga, that the elongated ovals or cartouches in the hieroglyphic section of the Stone contained the royal name, in this case that of Ptolemy. Young's discoveries were not limited to the Rosetta Stone. In 1816, very ingeniously, if rather luckily, he identified from the copy of an inscription at Karnak the cartouche of Queen Berenike which was recorded side by side with the cartouche of her husband, King Ptolemy Soter. From these two names he had succeeded in correctly identifying the phonetic values of six signs, and partly correctly a further three signs, while he had wrongly identified four signs. In addition he correctly suggested that another cartouche must be that of King Tuthmosis III of the Eighteenth Dynasty, recognised the alphabetic hieroglyphs for f and t, the determinative used in Late texts at the end of feminine names and the notation of various numerals. In all he was able to equate either correctly or nearly correctly about eighty demotic words with their hieroglyphic equivalents and, with the help of the Greek

words, translate most of them. Young's manu-
script notebooks containing most of his work on
hieroglyphs during 1814–18 are in the Manu-
scripts Department of the British Library (Add.
MSS 27281–5).

Young communicated the results of his inves-
tigations to the French scholar Jean François
Champollion (1790–1832) and also published
them in an article in the *Supplement to the Encyclo-
paedia Britannica* (4th edition) in 1819. Yet two
years later Champollion still clung to the mis-
taken belief that hieroglyphs were symbolic
and without phonetic value as his article 'De
l'écriture des anciens Égyptiens' which he published in 1821 proves. But within a few months of
writing that article he received a copy of the bilingual inscription in hieroglyphs and Greek on
an obelisk and its base block excavated at
Philae in 1815 by W.J. Bankes. Bankes had
rightly deduced that one of the cartouches in
the hieroglyphic section spelled the name
Cleopatra and had noted this information in
the margin of the copy which eventually reached
Champollion. When Champollion compared the
new cartouche with the cartouche of Ptolemy on
the Rosetta Stone, he could see that they showed

three signs in common and occurred in the expected positions if the names Ptolemy and Cleopatra were spelled alphabetically. This was enough to persuade him to abandon his previous theory that hieroglyphs were mere symbols and to adopt the view that at least in some cases they had phonetic values. He knew that Young had reached this conclusion before him but he never admitted it in print.

In September 1822 Champollion presented his important *Lettre à M. Dacier relative à l'alphabet des hiéroglyphes phonétiques* in which he corrected and greatly enlarged the list of phonetic hieroglyphs drawn up by Young and correctly deciphered the hieroglyphic forms of the names and titles of most of the Roman emperors of Egypt. Between then and his early death he drew up a classified list of hieroglyphs, identified the names of many Egyptian kings and formulated a system of grammar and general decipherment. Whereas Young had been unable to make any substantial progress after finding the key to the problem of decipherment, Champollion went on to lay the foundations on which present knowledge of the language of the ancient Egyptians is based and is

Jean-François Champollion
(1790–1832).

rightly looked upon as the Father of the Decipherment of Hieroglyphs.

The decipherment of proper names, although
providing the key to the system of writing, would
not have led to an understanding of the Egyptian language without the assistance of Coptic, the
script and language of the Christian descendants
of the ancient Egyptians (see above, p. 7). While
still a youth Champollion had realised the im-

portance of Coptic for decipherment and had studied it to such good purpose that he was able to identify with their Coptic equivalents many of the Egyptian words which he had been able to read. In his studies of the Rosetta Stone inscription his knowledge of Coptic enabled him to deduce the phonetic values of many syllabic signs and to assign correct readings to many pictorial characters whose meanings were known to him from the Greek text.

The method of decipherment

It was correctly assumed that the elongated oval ⬭ , or cartouche, always contained a royal name. There was only one cartouche (repeated six times with slight modifications) in the hieroglyphic section of the Rosetta Stone, and this was assumed to contain the name of Ptolemy because it was certain from the Greek section that the inscription concerned a Ptolemy. It was also assumed that if the cartouche did contain the name Ptolemy then the hieroglyphic characters in it would represent the sounds of the Greek letters and that all together they would represent the Greek from of the name Ptolemy. The obelisk and base block which W.J. Bankes had brought back from Philae to his home at Kingston Lacy in Dorset had on them a bilingual inscription in Greek and hieroglyphs. In the Greek section on the base block two royal names, those of Ptolemy and Cleopatra, were mentioned and in the hieroglyphic section on the obelisk two cartouches occurred close together, and these were therefore assumed to contain the hieroglyphic equivalents of these two names. When

these cartouches were compared with the cartouche on the Rosetta Stone, it was seen that one
of them contained signs which were almost identical with those in the Rosetta Stone cartouche.
Consequently, there was good reason to believe
that the cartouche on the Rosetta Stone and one
of those on the Bankes obelisk contained the
name 'Ptolemy' written in hieroglyphic characters. The forms of the cartouches in question are:

On the Rosetta Stone

On the Bankes obelisk

In the second of these cartouches the single sign
takes the place of the three signs at
the end of the first cartouche. The cartouche on
the Bankes obelisk which was thought to contain
the Egyptian equivalent of the name Cleopatra
appeared in this form:

Putting one above the other the cartouches be-
lieved to contain the names Ptolemy and Cleo-

patra on the Bankes obelisk and numbering the signs produces:

A   Ptolemy   (cartouche with numbered signs 1-14)

B   Cleopatra   (cartouche with numbered signs 1-11)

It will be seen at once that A1 and B5 are identical, and from their position in the names they must represent the letter P. A4 and B2 are also identical and from their position must represent the letter L. Since L is the second letter in the name Cleopatra, the sign B1 (⊿) must represent the letter K (Kleopatra in Greek). Since the values of signs B1, 2 and 5 are known in the cartouche of Cleopatra, they can be substituted in the following manner:

(cartouche with signs labelled K L 3 4 P 6 7 8 9 10 11)

In the Greek form of the name Cleopatra there are two vowels between the letters L and P and in the hieroglyphic form there are two signs ∫ and ∫, so it may be assumed that ∫ = E and ∫ = O. In some forms of the cartouche of Cleopatra B7(⌒) is replaced by ⌒which is identical with A2 and B10.

Since T is the second letter in the name Ptolemy and the seventh in the name Cleopatra, it can be assumed that ⟳ and ⌢ have substantially the same sound and that the sound is T. In the Greek form of the name Cleopatra there are two A's whose position agrees with B6 and B9 so it may be assumed that 𝕴 has the value of A. If these values are substituted for the hieroglyphs in B, the result is:

K L E O P A T ⟳ A ⌢ ◯

Of the remaining signs the last two (◌) had been interpreted almost correctly by early decipherers as a feminine termination. Thomas Young, however, more correctly took the group to be the determinative of the names of goddesses, queens and princesses. Now the only sign still requiring a phonetic equivalent is B8 (⌢); by elimination it must represent the letter R. If this value is inserted into the cartouche of Cleopatra, the whole name is deciphered. If the values learned from the cartouche of Cleopatra are applied to the cartouche of Ptolemy, the following results are obtained:

P T O L ⟳ ⌥ ⫴ ∶⌐ ⌁ ⟿ T P T ⌁ ▱

It can now be seen that the cartouche must be that of Ptolemy, but it is also clear that there are a number of hieroglyphs within the cartouche which do not actually form a part of the name. There are other forms of the cartouche of Ptolemy found on the Rosetta Stone, the simplest being: ⬭ . It is therefore evident that the other signs ⬭ are royal epithets corresponding to those in the Greek text meaning 'living for ever, beloved of Ptah'. The Greek form of Ptolemy, that is Ptolemaios, ends with an S, and it can therefore be assumed that the last sign in the simplest form of the cartouche as given above has the phonetic value S. The only hieroglyphs now remaing are ═ and ⟨⟨, and their positions in the name Ptolemy suggest that their phonetic values must be M and some vowel in which the sound I predominates. These values arrived at by guesswork and deduction by the earliest decipherers were applied to other cartouches, for example:

I 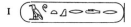   2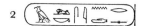

The Bankes obelisk at Kingston Lacy, Dorset.

The harbour of Rosetta as it is today.

In 1 it is possible to write down the values of all the signs except one, namely ℓ. Since the other signs spell out A-TKRTR, it is clear that the whole is the Greek title Autocrator and the previously unread sign must be U. In 2 only some of the hieroglyphs are known. By substitution the following is obtained:

A L ▱ S E 〜〜〜 T R ⟶

It is known that ⁓occurs in the name Berenike and represents the letter N. ⁓is the last sign in the hieroglyphic writing of 'Kaisaros', that is Caesar, and therefore represents the sound of S. Some of the cartouches containing variant forms of Cleopatra written in hieroglyphs begin with the sign ⁓, and it is clear that its phonetic value must be K. If these values are inserted in the above cartouche, the result is:

$$\text{A L K S E N T R S}$$

which is clearly meant to represent the name Alexandros, that is Alexander.

However, the problem of the signs at the end of the longer form of the cartouche of Ptolemy remained. Even though it might have been assumed that they represent the royal epithets 'living for ever, beloved of Ptah', this assumption remained to be proved. In Coptic it was known that the word for 'life' or 'living' was *onkh,* which was thought to be derived from an ancient Egyptian word *ankh* represented by the sign ☥. It was therefore guessed that the next signs ⁓meant 'ever'. Here Coptic was of little help for the ancient Egyptian word did not survive. However, the

first sign ┐ also appeared in a group of hieroglyphs known from Greek to mean 'called' or
'nick-named' which in Coptic began with the letter pronounced DJ. Since the second sign ᗡ was
known to have the phonetic value T the word
'ever' was surmised to have the sound value DJET.
The third sign═is a 'determinative' (see below, p.
61) and was not pronounced. Thus the first ep-
ithet means 'living (for) ever'.

  Of the remaining signs the first has the
phonetic value P and the second T, that is the first
two letters of the name of the god Ptah; the third
sign must therefore have the value of some sort
of H. If the signs form the name of Ptah, then
the sign which follows must mean 'beloved'. Here
again Coptic helped early decipherers to assign a
phonetic value to═, for the Coptic word meaning
'to love' is *mere* so it was assumed that the phonetic
value of the sign was mer. It should be pointed out
at this juncture that many of the values assigned
to hieroglyphs by the early decipherers were pre-
cisely correct only in the context of the writing of
Greek names in the Egyptian script. In classical
Egyptian hieroglyphs the sign═actually represents the value D, not T; similarly,◿ is not K, but
closer to Q. Champollion appreciated this weak-

ness in his initial attempts at interpretation, and he took the problem into account in his subsequent work. Consequently, by comparison of texts containing variant forms and skilful use of his knowledge of Coptic, Champollion succeeded in formulating the system of decipherment of Egyptian hieroglyphs which is substantially in use today.

The contents of the Rosetta Stone

The inscription on the Rosetta Stone is a copy of
the decree passed by a general council of priests
chosen by the Egyptian clergy from all parts of
Egypt which assembled at Memphis on the first
anniversary of the coronation of Ptolemy v Epiphanes, King of all Egypt. The young king had
been crowned in the eighth year of his reign, and
the first commemoration of the coronation consequently took place in his ninth year; the actual
date is 27 March 196 BC. During the Ptolemaic
Period most official documents must have been
provided in Greek and Egyptian versions because the ruling house and chief officers of
government were not Egyptian but Macedonian
Greek. The Ptolemies were all descended from
Ptolemy the son of Lagus, a general of Alexander
the Great, who first acted as Satrap of Egypt
after Alexander's death on behalf of Alexander's
half-brother Philip Arrhidaeus and then on
behalf of Alexander's son. By 305 BC both Philip
and Alexander's son were dead and Ptolemy was
strong enough to hold Egypt in his own right as

*The inscription at Rosetta commemorating the discovery
of the Rosetta Stone.*

his share of Alexander's empire. He took the name of Ptolemy I Soter (Saviour).

It is almost impossible to tell whether the decree was drawn up first in Greek or in Egyptian, although the rendering of one particular word in the Egyptian and Greek sections would rather suggest that the demotic version came first. In the passage concerning the shrine of Ptolemy Epiphanes, and in particular the diadems, crowns and hieroglyphic symbols upon it, the Greek version is extremely abbreviated and without the great detail given in the Egyptian versions. The Greek passage uses the words 'on the square surface' when identifying the location of the hieroglyphs and does not, therefore, seem to give a great deal of sense. The demotic version has 'on the upper side of the Atef crown' and the corresponding hieroglyphs read 'on the upper part of the *ḥp.t*'. The word *ḥp.t* has no determinative (see below, p. 60) and so could have a number of meanings of which one of the rarer is a type of crown. The original object represented by the biliteral hieroglyph (see below, p. 60) with the sound value *ḥp* () has never been satisfactorily identified, though it does look in its Late form rather like an open-

Old walls at Rosetta of the kind into which the Rosetta Stone was once incorporated.

sided right-angled set-square. The Greek word used in the Rosetta Stone passage is 'tetragon' which commonly means 'a square'. It is, therefore, possible that the hieroglyphic word really means a type of crown as in the demotic section and was misunderstood as a word connected with 'square' and so was misinterpreted in the Greek. Even if the original draft was in demotic, it would still have required approval by the Greek chancellery and any alterations would have been incorporated into the demotic original before a hieroglyphic version could have been made.

The text concerns the honours bestowed upon Ptolemy v by the temples of Egypt in return for the services rendered by him to Egypt both at home and abroad. Priestly privileges, especially those of an economic nature, are listed in great detail.

THE GREEK SECTION
OF THE
ROSETTA STONE

Note: It has not always been possible to divide the lines of the English translation exactly in accordance with the lines of the Greek text.

1. In the reign of the young one who has succeeded his father in the kingship, lord of diadems, most glorious, who has established Egypt and is pious

2. towards the gods, triumphant over his enemies, who has restored the civilised life of men, lord of the Thirty Years Festivals,[1] even as Hephaistos[2] the Great, a king like the Sun,[3]

3. great king of the Upper and Lower countries;[4] offspring of the Gods Philopatores, one whom Hephaistos has approved, to whom the Sun has given victory, the living image of Zeus,[5] son of the Sun, PTOLEMY,

4. LIVING FOR EVER, BELOVED OF PTAH, in the ninth year, when Aetos son of Aetos was

priest of Alexander, and the Gods Soteres, and the Gods Adelphoi, and the Gods Euergetai, and the Gods Philopatores[6] and

5. the God Epiphanes Eucharistos; Pyrrha daughter of Philinos being Athlophoros of Berenike Euergetis; Areia daughter of Diogenes being Kanephoros of Arsinoe Philadelphos; Irene

6. daughter of Ptolemy being Priestess of Arsinoe Philopator;[7] the fourth of the month of Xandikos, according to the Egyptians the 18th Mekhir.

DECREE. There being assembled the Chief Priests and Prophets and those who enter the inner shrine for the robing of the

7. gods, and the Fan-bearers and the Sacred Scribes and all the other priests from the temples throughout the land who have come to meet the king at Memphis, for the feast of the assumption

8. by PTOLEMY, THE EVER-LIVING, THE BELOVED OF PTAH, THE GOD EPIPHANES EUCHARISTOS, of the kingship in which he succeeded his father, they being assembled in the temple in Memphis on this day declared:

9. Whereas king PTOLEMY, THE EVER LIVING, THE
   BELOVED OF PTAH, THE GOD OF EPIPHANES
   EUCHARISTOS, the son of King Ptolemy and
   Queen Arsinoe, the Gods Philopatores, has
   been a benefactor both to the temples and

10. to those who dwell in them, as well as all those
    who are his subjects, being a god sprung from
    a god and goddess (like Horus the son of Isis
    and Osiris, who avenged his father Osiris)[8]
    (and) being benevolently disposed towards

11. the gods, has dedicated to the temples reve-
    nues in money and corn and has undertaken
    much outlay to bring Egypt into prosperity,
    and to establish the temples,

12. and has been generous with all his own
    means; and of the revenues and taxes levied
    in Egypt some he has wholly remitted and
    others has lightened, in order that the people
    and all the others might be

13. in prosperity during his reign; and whereas
    he has remitted the debts to the crown being
    many in number which they in Egypt and in
    the rest of the kingdom owed; and whereas
    those who were

14. in prison and those who were under accusa-
    tion for a long time, he has freed of the

charges against them; and whereas he has directed that the gods shall continue to enjoy the revenues of the temples and the yearly allowances given to them, both of

15. corn and money, likewise also the revenue assigned to the gods from vine land and from gardens and the other properties which belonged to the gods in his father's time;

16. and whereas he directed also, with regard to the priests, that they should pay no more as the tax for admission to the priesthood than what was appointed them throughout his father's reign and until the first year of his own reign; and has relieved the members of the

17. priestly orders from the yearly journey to Alexandria; and whereas he has directed that impressment for the navy shall no longer be employed; and of the tax on byssus[9] cloth paid by the temples to the crown he

18. has remitted two-thirds; and whatever things were neglected in former times he has restored to their proper condition, having a care how the traditional duties shall be fittingly paid to the gods;

19. and likewise has apportioned justice to all, like

Hermes[10] the great and great; and has or-
dained that those who return of the warrior
class, and of others who were unfavourably

20. disposed in the days of the disturbances,[11]
should, on their return be allowed to occupy
their old possessions; and whereas he provided that cavalry and infantry forces and
ships should be sent out against those who in-
vaded

21. Egypt by sea and by land, laying out great
sums in money and corn in order that the
temples and all those who are in the land
might be in saftey; and having

22. gone to Lycopolis[12] in the Busirite nome,
which had been occupied and fortified
against a siege with an abundant store of
weapons and all others supplies (seeing that
disaffection was now of long

23. standing among the impious men gathered
into it, who had perpetrated much damage to
the temples and to all the inhabitants of
Egypt), and having

24. encamped against it, he surrounded it with
mounds and trenches and elaborate fortifi-
cations; when the Nile made a great rise in the

eight year (of his reign), which usually floods the

25. plains, he prevented it, by damming at many points the outlets of the channels (spending upon this no small amount of money), and setting cavalry and infantry to guard

26. them, in a short time he took the town by storm and destroyed all the impious men in it, even as Hermes and Horus, the son of Isis and Osiris, formerly subdued the rebels in the same

27. district;[13] and as to those who had led the rebels in the time of his father and who had disturbed the land and done wrong to the temples, he came to Memphis to avenge

28. his father and his own kingship, and punished them all as they deserved, at the time that he came there to perform the proper ceremonies for the assumption of the crown; and whereas he remitted what

29. was due to the crown in the temples up to his eighth year, being no small amount of corn and money; so also the fines for the byssus

30. cloth not delivered to the crown, and of those delivered, the several fees for their verifica-

tion, for the same period; and he also freed the temples of (the tax of) the *artabe*[14] for every *aroura*[15] of sacred land and likewise

31. the jar of wine for each *aroura* of vine land; and whereas he bestowed many gifts upon Apis and Mnevis and upon the other sacred animals in Egypt, because he was much more considerate than the kings before him of all that belonged to

32. the gods; and for their burials he gave what was suitable lavishly and splendidly, and what was regularly paid to their special shrines, with sacrifices and festivals and other customary observances;

33. and he maintained the honours of the temples and Egypt according to the laws; and he adorned the temple of Apis with rich work, spending upon it gold and silver

34. and precious stones, no small amount; and whereas he has founded temples and shrines and altars, and has repaired those requiring it, having the spirit of a beneficent god in matters pertaining to

35. religion; and whereas after enquiry he has been renewing the most honourable of the temples during his reign, as is becoming; in

requital of which things the gods have given him health, victory and power, and all other good things,

36. and he and his children shall retain the kingship for all time. WITH PROPITIOUS FORTUNE: It was resolved by the priests of all the temples in the land to increase greatly the existing honours of

37. King PTOLEMY, THE EVER-LIVING, THE BELOVED OF PTAH, THE GOD EPIPHANES EUCHARISTOS, likewise of those of his parents the Gods Philopatores, and of his ancestors, the Gods Euergetai and

38. the Gods Adelphoi and the Gods Soteres and to set up in the most prominent place of every temple an image of the EVER-LIVING King PTOLEMY, THE BELOVED OF PTAH, THE GOD EPIPHANES EUCHARISTOS,

39. an image which shall be called that of 'PTOLEMY, the defender of Egypt', beside which shall stand the principal god of the temple, handing him the weapon of victory,[16] all of which shall be manufactured (in the Egyptian)

40. fashion; and that the priests shall pay homage to the images three times a day, and put

upon them the sacred garments, and perform the other usual honours such as are
given to the other gods in the Egyptian

41. festivals; and to establish for King PTOLEMY,
THE GOD EPIPHANES EUCHARISTOS, sprung of
King Ptolemy and Queen Arsinoe, the Gods
Philopatores, a statue and golden shrine in
each of the

42. temples, and to set it up in the inner chamber
with the other shrines; and in the great festivals in which the shrines are carried in
procession the shrine of the GOD EPIPHANES
EUCHARISTOS shall be carried in procession
with them.

43. And in order that it may be easily distin-
guishable now and for all time, there shall be
set upon the shrine the ten gold diadems of
the king, to which shall be added a uraeus[17]
but instead of

44. the uraeus-shaped diadems which are upon
the other shrines, in the centre of them shall
be the crown called *Pschent*[18] which he put on
when he went into the temple at Memphis

45. to perform therein the ceremonies for as-
suming the kingship; and there shall be
placed on the square surface round about the

diadems, beside the aforementioned crown, golden symbols (eight in number signifying)
46. that it is (the shrine) of the king who makes manifest the Upper and the Lower countries. And since it is the 30th of Mesore on which the birthday of the king is celebrated, and likewise (the 17th of Paophi)
47. on which he succeeded his father in the kingship, they have held these days in honour as name-days in the temples, since they are sources of great blessings for all; it was further decreed that a festival shall be kept in the temples throughout Egypt
48. on these days in every month, on which there shall be sacrifices and libations and all the ceremonies customary at the other festivals (and the offerings shall be given to the priests who)
49. serve in the temples. And a festival shall be kept for King PTOLEMY, THE EVERLIVING, THE BELOVED OF PTAH, THE GOD EPIPHANES EU-CHARISTOS, yearly in the temples throughout the
50. land from the 1st of Thoth for five days, in which they shall wear garlands and perform sacrifices and libations and the other usual

honours, and the priests (in each temple) shall be called

51. priests of the GOD EPIPHANES EUCHARISTOS in addition to the names of the other gods whom they serve; and his priesthood shall be entered upon all formal documents (and engraved upon the rings which they wear);

52. and private individuals shall also be allowed to keep the festival and set up the aforementioned shrine and have it in their homes, performing the aforementioned celebrations

53. yearly, in order that it may be known to all that the men of Egypt magnify and honour the GOD EPIPHANES EUCHARISTOS the king, according to the law. This decree shall be inscribed on a stela of

54. hard stone in sacred [that is hieroglyphic] and native [that is demotic] and Greek characters and set up in each of the first, second and third [rank] temples beside the image of the ever-living king.

Notes

1. The Sed Festival, originally held at thirty-year intervals after a king's coronation, in order to renew a king's physical powers.
2. In the Egyptian version Ptah.
3. In the Egyptian version Ra.
4. The South and North of Egypt, the two great predynastic kingdoms, were always remembered in the royal title.
5. In the Egyptian version Amun.
6. Alexander the Great, Ptolemy I and Berenike I, Ptolemy II and Arsinoe II, and Ptolemy III and Berenike II, and Ptolemy IV and Arsinoe III respectively.
7. Eponymous priests: priests and priestesses, always with Greek names, attached to the royal cult, who served in their office for a year and were arranged in two colleges in a completely Greek institution.
8. Ie Horus-avenger-of-his-father, in Greek Harendotes.
9. Fine linen.
10. In the Egyptian version Thoth.
11. A reference to the years since 205 BC, during which Upper Egypt had been ruled by two rebel native pharaohs, first Hor-Wennefer (previously misread as Hor-em-akhet) and, since 199 BC, Ankh-Wennefer (misread as Ankh-em-akhet).
12. A town in the ninth nome (administrative area) of the Delta, probably near Busiris but not identified with certainty.
13. According to one version of the Osiris legend, his followers under Horus and Thoth defeated the supporters of Seth nearby at Hermopolis Parva.
14. A measure of grain.

15. A measurement of land equal to about ⅔ of an acre (about 2,735 sq. m).

16. The *khepesh*, or scimitar, the royal weapon often depicted being given by a god to the king.

17. The cobra, symbol of kingship.

18. From the Egyptian *Pa-sekhemty*, the two powers, that is the Double Crown which incorporated the Red Crown of Lower Egypt and the White Crown of Upper Egypt.

THE ANCIENT
EGYPTIAN LANGUAGE

Early decipherment was not all quite as straight-
forward as transliterating names and epithets
would suggest. By the Ptolemaic Period hieroglyphs were virtually fossilised so that the vocabulary and grammar which they were used to
express bore little resemblance to the vocabulary
and grammar embodied in contemporary demotic. In the hieroglyphic section of the Rosetta
Stone, for example, the word used for 'king' is the
title which dates back to the beginning of the Dy-
nastic Period, namely 'he of the reed and bee'.
Since the reed was the symbol of Upper Egypt,
that is all of Egypt south of the Delta, and the bee
symbolised Lower Egypt, that is the Delta, the title meant its holder was ruler of all Egypt. In the
demotic section, however, the word used is 'phar-
aoh', literally 'the great house, or the palace',
which by extension had come to mean since the
New Kingdom the person who resided in the palace, that is the king. In the hieroglyphic section the
Greeks are denoted by the ancient term *Haw nebu,*

that is '(Aegean) Islanders', whereas in demotic they are called *Wynn,* a term for Ionian, because the Eastern Greeks were the ones with whom the Egyptians of the Late Period had most contact. A simple but good example of the differences between the hieroglyphic and demotic texts can be found in the ways the words 'stela of hard stone' are rendered. The hieroglyphic version has *ahay* (stela) *nty* (of) *aat* (stone) *rudj* (hard); the demotic, *wyt* (stela) *iny* (stone) *djery* (hard).

Nevertheless, scholars were able to establish that hieroglyphs can be divided into two categories, phonograms or sound signs, and ideograms or sense signs. In fact some hieroglyphs can be phonograms or ideograms in different circumstances. Of phonetic hieroglyphs, which are used to spell words, some are 'alphabetic' like ▫ *(h),* ⌡ *(b),* ⌐ *(f),* 𝕝*(m),* ▣*(g)*; others are biliteral, having a root of two consonants, like ☞ *(gm),* ☒ *(wn),* ⊐ *(pr)*; some are triliteral, with three consonants, like ⌡ *(nfr),* ▭ *(htp),* ⟋ *(sdm)*. Egyptian scripts show no true vowels, only semi-vowels or weak consonants, namely ⌡*(i),* ⌡⌡ *(y),* ⌡ *(w)*; the two non-English semi-vocalic sounds 𝕝 *(3)* and ⌐ (') are often represented as *a*.

Ideograms signify either the actual object, for example ☉ 'sun' or 〰 'hill-country', in which case they are usually followed by a single stroke ❘: for example ⊕ 'sun'; or if feminine a *t* (⌒) and a stroke: for example 〰 'hill-country'. Or else they signify an idea closely associated with the pictorial object. Thus the sun (☉) can represent 'day'; or a scribe's writing equipment (⾗) can represent 'scribe' or 'write'. By extension ideograms can act as determinatives for words spelled out phonetically. Thus the sun(☉) can be the determinative for ⌇☉*rk*, 'time', ⦚⌇☉ *wbn*, 'to shine', or ⦚⌇☉ *3t*, 'moment'. A boat on water(⥃)can be used as the determinaitve for words like ⬭⥃ *dpt*, 'boat', ⬭⥃ *ḥd*, 'sail north' or ⥃⦚⥃ *iw(y)*, 'to be boatless'. Sometimes in the case of homonyms (words of similar sound) only the determinative makes clear the meaning intended. Thus ⦚⌇ *nfrt* with varying determinatives can mean 'good things' (⬭), 'cattle' (⬭), 'beautiful women' (⬭), 'a name of the Underworld' (〰) or 'the tomb' (⬭).

Both biliteral and triliteral signs are usually accompanied by alphabetic hieroglyphs expressing part or the whole of their sound value. Sometimes this so-called phonetic complement is un-

necessary as in the writing ⸑⸑ which reads *nfr*, not
nfrfr. But it is generally necessary in words written with a sign capable of more than one phonetic
reading like the sign ⸑ which can be read *mr* or *3b*.
The phonetic complement makes quite clear
which reading is to be used, either ⸑⸑ or ⸑⸑.

A sample hieroglyphic sentence shows how all
these elements work.

kt	nt	tm	rdỉ	pr	hf3w	m	b3b3w
ket	net	tem	redi	per	hefau	em	babau

'Another (remedy) for preventing from coming
out a snake from (its) hole.' Hieroglyphic inscriptions (like texts written in the hieratic and demotic scripts) are commonly read from right to
left. For reasons of design they can also be written
from left to right, or in vertical columns read from
top to bottom. Normally an inscription is read
from the direction in which signs representing
living creatures are looking. In the sentence
quoted above the creatures look left, so the text is
read from the left to the right.

THE HIEROGLYPHIC ALPHABET

From what has been said above it will be clear that it is not possible, strictly speaking, to compile an 'alphabet' of hieroglyphic signs. For practical purposes, however, certain uniliteral hieroglyphs have been selected to form a kind of 'alphabet' which is universally used for the organisation of dictionaries, word lists, indexes and for general reference purposes. It runs as follows:

Sign	Transcription	Sound value
🦅	(vulture) ꜣ	Glottal stop (as in 'bottle' when pronounced by a Cockney)
𓇋	(flowering reed) i	I
𓇌	(two flowering reeds) y	Y
\\\\	(oblique strokes) y	Y
▬◗	(forearm and hand) ꜥ	Ayin of the Semitic languages
🐤	(quail chick) w	W
℮	(cursive development of 🐤) w	W
⌟	(foot) b	B
▢	(stool) p	P
⌐	(horned viper) f	F
🦉	(owl) m	M

﹀﹀	(water) *n*	N
◯	(mouth) *r*	R
⊓	(reed shelter) *h*	H
⌇	(wick of twisted flax) *ḥ*	slightly guttural *h*
⊜	*(placenta?)* *ḫ*	CH (as in loch)
●	(animal's belly) *ẖ*	slightly softer than *h*
—	(door bolt) *s*	S
⌇	*(folded cloth)* *s*	S
▭	*(pool)* *š*	SH
△	(hill) *ḳ*	Q
⌒	(basket with handle) *k*	K
⊟	(jar-stand) *g*	G (as in goat)
⌒	(loaf) *t*	T
▭	(tethering rope) *ṯ*	Tj
⌒	(hand) *d*	D
⌐	(snake) *ḏ*	Dj